This edition published by Ravette Publishing 2007.

ISBN 13: 978-1-84161-283-6

ЯR
RAVETTE PUBLISHING

Born to Shop, Shop, Shop, Shop, Shop, Shop, Shop

Let me

Shop for Shoes

 and 

nobody

gets hurt

Whoever said
money can't buy you
happiness didn't
know where to
shop

If the shoe
fits, buy it
in every
colour

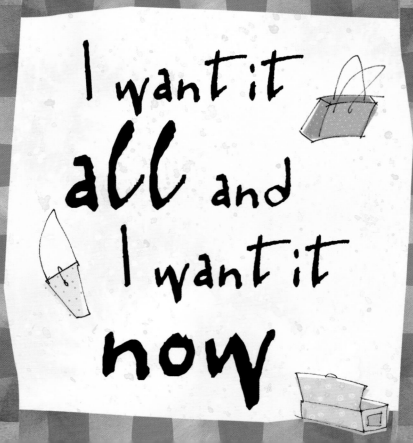

My husband says he'll leave me if I carry on shopping, Lord I'll miss that man

Too much
of a good
thing is
wonderful

Born free now I'm expensive

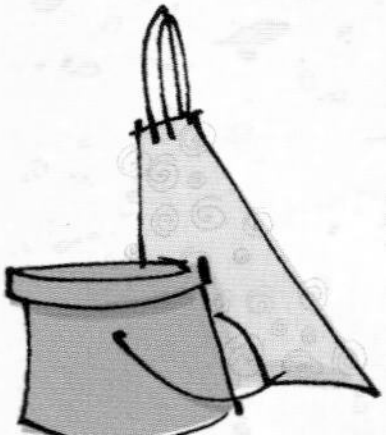

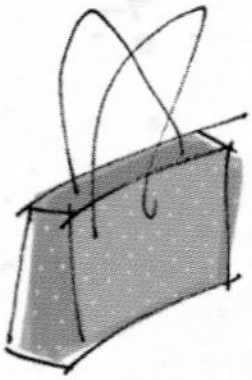

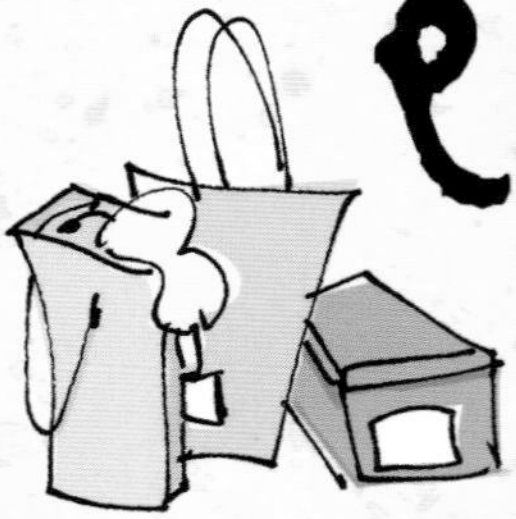

Lead me not into temptation, I can find the way myself

Friends are like shoes, you can never have enough

Whenever I get the winter blues I shop for shoes

I need therapy... retail therapy

Born to **Shop** whatever the weather

Born to **Shop**, forced to **Cook**

You can't have too many friends, or pairs of shoes

Born
to
Shop
non stop

Other BORN TO SHOP titles available ...

	ISBN	Price
All men are created equal... equally useless	978-1-84161-257-7	£4.99
Another day in paradise	978-1-84161-255-3	£4.99
100% gorgeous ... most of the time!	978-1-84161-284-3	£4.99
Friends are the family we choose for ourselves	978-1-84161-254-6	£4.99
I never met a calorie I didn't like	978-1-84161-256-0	£4.99
Life's too short to drink bad wine	978-1-84161-275-1	£4.99
'M' is for Mother, not for Maid	978-1-84161-274-4	£4.99

HOW TO ORDER   Please send a cheque/postal order in £ sterling, made payable to 'Ravette Publishing' for the cover price of the books and allow the following for post & packaging ...

UK & BFPO	70p for the first book & 40p per book thereafter
Europe & Eire	£1.30 for the first book & 70p per book thereafter
Rest of the world	£2.20 for the first book & £1.10 per book thereafter

RAVETTE PUBLISHING LTD
Unit 3 Tristar Centre, Star Road, Partridge Green, West Sussex RH13 8RA
Tel: 01403 711443   Fax: 01403 711554   Email: ravettepub@aol.com

Prices and availability are subject to change without prior notice.